Learning Curve

Poems

Helga Kidder

BLUE LIGHT PRESS
1st WORLD PUBLISHING

San Francisco | Fairfield | Delhi

Learning Curve

Helga Kidder

Copyright ©2021 by Helga Kidder

First Edition.

ISBN: 978-1-4218-3713-0

Library of Congress Cataloging-in-Publication Data

1ST WORLD LIBRARY
PO Box 2211
Fairfield, Iowa 52556
www.1stworldpublishing.com

BLUE LIGHT PRESS
www.bluelightpress.com
Email: bluelightpress@aol.com

Author photo: Everett Kidder

Cover art: charcoal on paper by Lauren Kidder

Das Wort
wird doch nur
andre Worte nach sich ziehn,
Satz den Satz.
So moechte Welt,
endgueltig,
sich aufdraengen,
schon gesagt sein.
Sagt sie nicht.

Ingeborg Bachmann, "Ihr Worte"

CONTENTS

I.

II.

III.

IV.

I.

Between Tongues

How many words are in a language?
After six weeks of listening, layering words,
stacking them into piles
in rooms wall-papered with my first language,
I spoke my first full English sentence.

The dichotomy similar to knit and purl,
the wrong and right sides of meaning,
or two trees with many branches,
each wanting to grow its own direction.
Words flocking to me like birds,
then flitting back to a branch.

A new language, as if I had put on
an overcoat, still dreaming in German.
Forever rooted in the language
I was born into, assembling and moving words
on the conveyor belt of knowledge.

I corral sentences like horses,
train them with daily exercises,
watch Saturday morning cartoons
or *Password*, dictionary in lap.
Ears always open to new sounds,
new meanings, such as *nip it in the bud,*
catty corner, a pone of corn in its sack.

When will I be fluent?
Years jumbled both languages inside me.
Utterings reverted to childhood,
leaving me to balance the tightrope
of speech and understanding
suspended between two continents.

LOEWENGASSE

Only rain kept us off this dirt road
running along the prison wall
as summer dragged house shadows
through the afternoon. The only girl,
I kicked the ball with boys, braids flying.
We loved the ball, its roll and leap
into the air like wishes. We ran
and kicked, scuffed shoes,
lifted dirt all afternoon, our yelps
and screams bouncing off the brick.
Oblivious to neighbors hanging shirts
on a line or ladling milk into a pail
or cobbling wood for a shelf,
we learned to cope with the world,
shuffling the ball between feet,
our futures.

AFTER THE WAR

The woman who fled the communists
lived next door, knitted for money.
Once she ran out of green wool,
and I had to wear a cardigan
with half of the sleeves shades darker.

But in the abandoned house beside the church
lived a witch, mother and neighbors gossiped.
Behind the second-floor window,
glass grayed and smudged,
we imagined her hexing passers-by.
At night we listened to the house
confessing her spells.

When my sister spilled oatmeal soup on my foot,
she cried into mother's apron
as the nurse popped the blisters.
That was after Dieter Gertz,
standing on top of a wagon,
gunned my head with rocks
and for six weeks the bandage turned me
into a mummy.

On better days we climbed the saints
chiseled into the church walls,
saw the cobbler's beard shake warnings
as we tried to blow out the eternal light
burning among the apostles
defending Jesus on the Mount of Olives.

When all church bells rang and shook
the dishes in the cupboard, we knew
a soul had been saved from the witch.
To celebrate we sprinkled sugar on wet bread,
crossed our foreheads with holy water.

What could we believe
when witches and saints lived next to each other.

If I Were a Bird

I could fly away
to the forest,
open my throat
to the third-heaven language,
let my words collect
in clouds and rise
over you like a blessing.

If I could un-do time,
let it settle in my wings,
feather it,
spread it out like seeds
in rows, I'd pick
one at a time
for a hundred years.

If I could re-do the moments
in a wheatfield,
golden for harvest,
we would know each other
again
and remember
how love satisfies.

If soldiers didn't have to die,
and you'd be a leaf,
spring-green,
I'd perch next to you

on a branch
in the forest of my world
and sing for you
the song of un-doing.

RITUAL 1950

Each Saturday my sister brought home
a bag full of eight milk buns
left over from that morning.
Her hair a halo like a saint's.

> *Oilcloth-dressed table.*
> *Half a ring of Fleischwurst,*
> *quarter pound of Swiss cheese,*
> *mustard. Pot of tea,*
> *steaming.*

As the window darkened,
we could hear footsteps
that should have been father's,
until she exhaled, slumped
into the last chair.
Mother unrumpled the bag
with a smile, portioned
the buns onto our plates.
We feasted, an empress
and her princesses.

To the Body, All

– after Lisel Mueller

I watch myself like a sister,
like clouds converging.
I am the movie star,
the princess, Time magazine's
most eligible heiress.
I own my kingdom,
the small study,
all the words in books,
the screen parades all underlings
into my domain
that I shut off at will.
I am the pianist,
the prophet,
one of the chosen
that fits into the universal plan,
the way a bluebird's flight is set.
I want the heart to tell me
how long I will breathe,
how long the lilac will bloom.
I am the daughter of the moon
living above disasters, diseases,
shedding earth's burdens.
I eat the food of the dead,
the sugars that bind the soul
to the body, all the bread.
I drink the wines, the sodas,
wait for the final crescendo of drums,
violins, and the trumpet's blare.

FATHER'S LOVE

The day comes when each of us
is overloved, whether by a god
or mortal father.

J. Allyn Rosser

I still pretend scenes with the father
I never knew. But he knew me
at birth and until I was three.

Surely, he carried me in his arms
when I cried, fed me a bottle
or later with a spoon.

Surely, he bounced me on his knee,
sang a nursery rhyme, laughed
at my *Papa, Papa, more,*
and kissed my cheek.

Surely, he took me by the hand,
strolled me through the city park.
Look at the swans in the pond
and how the weeping willow
strokes the water.

Surely, he remembered me
in the next sixty years of his life,
my eyes and mouth like his
seeking to fulfill the longing
for love.

Surely, he realized the day
never came when I was overloved
by my father.

What Love Is

Though the sky was mostly blue
with relieving rain so flowers grew,
romance which you thought was love
has withered. No matter how hard
you loved, you think it has passed
through the wormhole of time,
it has fallen into the river of yesterdays
settling between pebbles and sand.
The stream of life flowed over it,
carried children, pets, and a job
that required your hands and heart.

But you watch a spider weave
its doilies in your garden,
a hummingbird whirring from bloom
to bloom, a blue-tailed lizard
whisking in and out of the brick wall,
and you smile. Even the rooms
you re-enter each morning,
the comfortable chair you nap in,
shelves stuffed with books,
sate your heart. And your feet
have learned to move forward,
step by step, toward your last love.

First Flight

. . . and in its shadow
we know one another

W. S. Merwin "The Rock"

Married one week, mid-air between
continents, hunger for anything new
quivered inside me like a leaf, unfurling.

The sky February blue.
Behind me a Black Forest village,
mother, and nosy neighbors.
In front of me a town in Tennessee
full of strangers speaking
in a strange language.

Below, ice floes on the ocean,
steaming like mother's kettle boiling
as the sun forced its way down.

I sat next to my new husband,
confident in a herringbone suit
mother helped pick out,
my white sling-backs daring
the 'not before Easter' rule.

We talked about our future,
children, the two-bedroom apartment
with bathroom waiting for us.
Among invisible stars we spoke
without shadows between our words.

I couldn't know fourteen years later,
I would trip over nutshells and twigs
scattered on the driveway
after strong winds shook trees,
leaving a taste of rain and divorce in the air.

Descending through clouds
this flight propelled me
into a new name, a new language,
a woman I would learn to be.

THE SIXTIES

Like a seed sprouting, I was all stem,
budding. My idols, Brigitte Bardot,
her baby-doll look, and in America
Jackie Kennedy in haute couture.

      I pledged allegiance to the flag

Miniskirt, go-go boots, or in summer
gingham jumper and daisy slip-ons.

Dress-up meant shift and coat ensemble,
pearl studs, pillbox, handbag, bow pumps.

      I raised the flag each time
        I spoke a new word
          in English

A time of Mary Quant and Bobbi Brown,
Carol Brent and Mizrahi.
A time for *Peyton Place* and *Dark Shadows*.

I flowered in pink, orange, forest green
and Merle Norman make-up, black eyeliner,
pale lipstick. It was all about eyes and knees,
about pierced ears.

I raised the flag
        when I asked neighbors
                for recipes, for potluck

Not flat-chested like Twiggy, I was a flower
in full bloom, folding out and opening
to the stamen, a Marilyn Monroe.

        I raised the flag when
                I listened to others, mingled
                        their thoughts with mine

I kept raising the flag each time I returned
from Germany to the Statue of Liberty,
breathed freedom.

MONDAY'S CHILD

I've not had a haircut in months,
wanting a mane that cascades down
my shoulders. I want the wind
to muss my hair so I can't see the world
and its ugliness. I want hair so strong
I could rival Samson, have hair
that extends my knowledge
all the way down to the split ends.

I'm thinking of Rita Hayworth
in Forties movies, her fiery red hair
inflaming all that came close to her.
I want hair that frames my face
like the angel's whose picture
graces my nightstand.
I want hair that veils my body
so everyone believes I'm a goddess,
so that my husband will comb my hair
and braid it for the night.

THE WORLD IS TOO MUCH WITH US

William Wordsworth

I don't remember the chain of my ancestry,
how I ended up with the round face
of a Neanderthal, the red strands of a Goth,
the skin of a Roman, and the temper of a Hun.
All of these nations in my blood
I carried to America.

I learned that buttons on your shirt may signal
pride, that hate is a common denominator,
that guns are toys in your play chest,
and the flick of a cigarette builds fires,
leaves houses and people and wildlife in ashes.

I carry with me half of the world,
some days feel the weight on my shoulders
like Atlas. That's why I don't mind
that leaves brittle and trees let go,
that air plays in bare branches.

THE HEART

Sometimes you flutter when I see my beloved
or beat a drum against the wall of my chest
in a quarrel. Sometimes you scatter rhythm
like seeds when I toss and turn.
                              I confide
my longings, my loves, my hates to you
on quiet evenings as we lounge in front of
the TV. Then at other times you spew them
out of me like a geyser.
                         You work diligently
and with confidence like a swiss watch
that ratchets the grooves of blades.

I see you inside me like a red bird tucking
his wings under, feathering my chest
with a tingle.
              You are my prime number,
my reason as you multiply breath.
You fruit my mind's orchard.

I dread the time when your warranty runs out,
when you blip, blip, then hum on the screen,
when your strength like that of a waterfall
trickles out between rocks.
                           Sometimes
nitroglycerin re-sprouts your fallow field.
Sometimes frost covers you in white.

BETWEEN SHADOWS

A lone bee hums and nuzzles blue salvia
as I water the garden,
                            fill the birdbath.

> *Routines tie to earth,*
> *keep us grounded.*

The morning enters like a lady-in-waiting,
fluffs her golden skirts.
                            One butterfly
breakfasts on pinky winkies.

Bee, butterfly where are your brothers, sisters?

> *Neglect and loss teach us*
> *how to live within ourselves.*

Like the moon – just a white sphere in blue.

The sun crisps leaves
of sweetgum and sourwood.
                            Haze
enfolds juniper and bay bushes.

> *We want to drink the day's nectar,*
> *not swallow promises forgotten.*

Wrens frenzy around the feeder
as I leave behind outside worries –

                                 fate –

enter the house of shadows

                        and light.

THE DOOR

– after Mark Strand

Always a door that needs opening.
Will it shriek or glide easily in its hinges?
A voice from behind you teases,

                          go, go.
You and your voice step willingly through.
No fear of a gun or a fist or knife.
No one's life in your hands.

Inside the door your breathing shallows.
Leaves swing-dance in the wind.
Birds and squirrels chatter for seeds.
Katydids playing wood instruments.

You step over cracked hickory nuts
and twigs from last night's storm
on your morning walk to the mailbox.
No news from the children is good news.

This room opened for you at birth.
Furnish and decorate it
with your life.

EVERY BREATH IS A GIFT

Our ancestors worshipped trees
                              because
they were not afraid to die
                              and begin again.
They branch out
                    when light
                              and enlightenment
grow sparse.
                    They root
                              deeper
when earth shakes
                              mountains and waves.
My grandfather felled Black Forest trees,
                                        spruce and fir,
built my cradle with sacred wood,
                                    gnarls and knots,
rocking me to sleep.
Scars, cracks, and bends only visible inside,
        the way we keep them inside
when we had to give in,
                        learned to let go of the self.
Heartwood at the center,
                          they moan and shake
their heads in gusts and gales.
                        We listen
        to the leaves whisper
                          ancient wisdoms

on sultry evenings,
        the branches
            inviting song.

POETRY

You were made to do hard things,
open the door to birch leaves
covering the porch with a gold carpet,
to tiny feathers left in the bird bath.
You may be clinging to a brittle branch
before it falls on me. There is no chart
or list to mark off, to allow a breather.
I know walls won't protect you
when the wind spins like a dreidel
through the woods. It may whirl you
against the trunk of trees, flatten
you against rocks. But this is not
your only home.
             When I look up,
I see you in a sliver of moon gliding
between stars, lighting the Milky Way
or some other universe that fills in
where you've been
               to keep me whole.

ACROBATICS

Through the night I re-live the day,
chores grinning from the yard,
a country girl lost in the maze
of a city, scientists laboring
over a cure for a pandemic.

At dawn my forehead spins
and nothing is solved.
I was born into love and worry,
the furrows of a field
I plow each day.

This morning I study the sky
expecting a meteor crashing
into the seashore, veiling the sun
with a shield of gas and smoke.

Instead, I see the belly of the moon
next to a star, day pushing them out
of the way for the sun's rays
waking leaves.

I was created in earth, heaving
and swelling passion to breathe.
These are my knees of pain,
my bone-thickened hands.
This is the bridge of memory,
the branches that net the sky
to catch everything that falls.

FALSE PEACE

Even my hair loosens without pulling,
woke me from turning in half-sleep
as one fine hair fell on my arm.

Perhaps a spirit had touched me,
pushing her fingertips through the dimensions
that create gaps between us.

Still in the world,
skin sloughs and builds tiny blisters,
browns in the sun who without barrier
grabs, wrinkles, and thins.

Let me praise the shirt that hides flaws
as my arms glide into their cottony tunnels,
their good will that buttons
over the mounds of my breast.

I enter this morning of fogged windows
from the soft hands of night rain,
creating a false peace,
calm as a cup of warm milk before sleep.

Dotted with flecks of doubt, I open my mouth
in a mirage of rain,
each drop slaking my parched throat.

Tell me mirror, do I love myself enough
to jump the hurdles of this day?

THE PATH

Luck is like a shard of sea glass
in the hand. Squeezed too hard,
blood will surface.
Life blood,
so easily raised
if we allow the cut.

Some people are born lucky,
the right color,
the right religion,
the right neighborhood
at the right time.

Each morning I tighten sheets,
wipe counters,
arrange the pink throats
of lilies in a vase.

Some people are born luckier.
At night my heart pretends
to hear only music,
forgets the gods
have tarred and feathered
the path, ignores
the splinter in my eye.

Mirror, Mirror on the Wall

You must have been disappointed as I was
eye to eye with the *Mona Lisa*,
that enigmatic smile Leonardo mastered
and now hangs in the Louvre, small
for its notoriety. And did you blush
like I did in Florence standing in front of
The Three Graces, naked in their gold frame
as if frolicking on a nude beach at the Baltic Sea?
And now James Bond is dead. The suave spy
wooed by slender models as he traveled
the globe, father to Indiana Jones, who wears
the same magnet in his pockets.

Paintings and movies grab my eyes like pictures
in an album left on the coffee table I browse
through sipping from a cup. But I usually get
side-tracked by cookies the English call biscuits.
Munching, I think of the next tennis stroke
my coach wants me to perfect. Which leads
to dumbbells I lift every Saturday to strengthen
my shoulders, to return the ball like a metaphor,
strong and certain of its power. Mostly, I preen
when standing in front of the mirror,
my soul naked and blank like a child's
drinking from the vat of life.

Stepping Through the Self

Mourning doves snag scarves of air,
peck seeds fallen onto the stone terrace.
They throw out their chests until all seeds
are gone, then fly off in a blue blur.

I seek sparkle in rings, necklaces,
that announce gaudy, slightly slutty thoughts
in a corner of my heart.
The stars' sheen fills my nights
and the moon's pull draws me into its shadows.

Each train arrives somewhere
stowed with baggage.
Pull the emergency brake at the moment
when we hold phantoms like lost limbs in our hands.

I sit in the sun to dry my hair,
shake my head as if denying
secrets hiding like dust in the folds of a dress
that still hangs in the closet.
Carry us on waves of doubt.
Comb our thoughts
through the rat's nest of blind belief.

Let us be like doves swallowing the good we find,
as we ride through discord
and tunnel winds. Let us be the sheen
floating in evening streets,
that golden beam of moon on a smoothed sea,
the world fringed in blue.

II.

My Hands

traveled far from my German cradle
to Tennessee, have fingered sheets while I slept,
held forks, spoons, and knives,
parted water,
learned to craft my thoughts into poems.

Fingers crooked and bony like soldiers
weary returning from the front,
nails lacking half-moons to dream in.
Not supple enough to play the piano softly,
more like Wagner's bold strokes
hammering out a melody.

I bite my nails to the quick, bite down hard
on life and splinter it between my teeth
in troubled times. But my hands
have wandered the anatomy of love,
and remember.

Now hours and days fall through my fingers,
an entire life, soon ghosts of memory
collected in thick knuckles,
tips destined to turn cold and blue.

Somewhere in Tennessee

I was here once before.
I breathed in the smell of damp grass
and soft earth, admired the horse's chestnut mane
as musk mingled with my wish
to step out of myself like my ancestors
when they first encountered wild horses
and how they fostered possibilities
of a different destiny.
                    I had it all planned
in my head, the way we anticipate
a wedding ceremony or take the host
on the tongue from a priest's hand.
It was that clear in my mind.
                            Yes,
it was a cool and sunny day.
I would hold out my hand with a carrot
the horse would gently take with his soft lips
and I would listen to the crunching between teeth.
My hand would then rub the distance
between muzzle and forehead,
and the large eyes would look at me
as it nuzzled my hand for more.
                        When I arrived
at the corral, a large sign said, *Don't feed the horse.*
I had it all planned, brought carrots.
I stroked the horse's forehead
as if it were the future looking at me
wishing to be fed.

BRUISED

All I can think of today is tomatoes.
>The red fruit some say Eve gave Adam.
Logically, that can't be true
>since it was a tree that stood in the Garden
and tomatoes don't grow on trees.
>Unless it was really a bush that centered Eden,
though the serpent may have had difficulty
>climbing a stalk without breaking it.

I think Eve was tempted by the bright-red color
>of the tomato, and when Adam bit into it,
the juice ran down his bare chest and stung.
>An apple would have been neater.

I'm reasoning that tomatoes need picking
>or they will let go and fall to earth.
Maybe it was not the serpent who willed Eve
>to pick the fruit but her common sense.

There is also the dispute whether a tomato is a fruit,
>and the Bible definitely refers to temptation
as a fruit.

This is what may have happened:
>Eve said to Adam, *I'm going to pick tomatoes
for a salad*, and he answered, *OK, but this time
>slice some onions as well into the vinegar
and oil dressing.*

Unfortunately, they were evicted
        as soon Eve tasted the salad and gave Adam
a bowl, so they had to go without dinner that night.

In retrospect, I don't think snakes like apples
        but tomatoes. As they fall to the ground,
their skins split, expose flesh,
        open themselves to the worm.

LEARNING CURVE

Leaves and wind dance in the driveway.
      A modern dance, zig-zag, lifting,
falling, a dance they study each year,
      then blush the ground.
                              Later
nimbostratus let go of snow
      that covers everything with a white quilt.
My dog's footprints inform
      another language
                        for rabbits and squirrels.

Reba, my colorist, calls me *Sweet Pea*
      reminding me of English peas sweetening
a lettuce and onion salad.
                        She sections
my hair expertly and runs the tip of the bottle
      along the grooves.
                        Ean takes lessons
in tennis. A nine-year-old, he whacks the ball,
      still thinks its force will win the game.
Like a mouse that runs the maze for a treat,
      he will learn understanding and skill.

In Switzerland the Matterhorn is the mountain
        to climb. In Japan it is Mt. Fuji.
On the trek we mark a walking stick every 10 yards,
        pass hikers squatting at the path's edge,
stopped by their limitations.
                                Shah Jahan built
the Taj Mahal after his wife died wishing
        with each curve of carved stone he'd shown
his love earlier.
                        I, too, hold myself back, not give
as much of myself as I used to.

Valentine's Day at the Krystal

Rain grays the sky, rhythms
windshield wipers into a swaying dance.
Cars and trucks rush through puddles,
wet-brushing grime and dust.

Forgetting the wet-dog smell
closing my umbrella,
I savor Krystal burgers and fries
reading pages of poetry,
relish the tang of pickles
like an unexpected metaphor.

How can clouds hold back rain
for days without bursting?
We are prisoners of cells
dying before returning to dust.
We are mystery
every time we touch dust,
eighty per cent of it human.

My chocolate wrapper's wisdom:
A gentle touch speaks volumes.
Touch as fine as spring rain,
touch like swells of waves on piano keys.
Taste the salt and sugar of skin.

SOUL SEARCH

Out of darkness
springs light
like a lion

pawing the tips
of the forest
glides

over leaves
trunks
to the roots

of the day
talons
spread out

until sun
fills
the sky

in us as song
of flesh
a lamp

serving
as shield
from harm

crouching
in shadows
that increase

furrow
our brows
until sunset

wraps itself
around us
and light hides

in our faces
and souls
through the night.

COLLECTION OF BLUES

The train's horn blows midnight into dreams,
of steel stairs I climbed long ago.
Slatted wood seats, air metal-tinged,
billows of engine smoke in the windows,
those early blues years magnified.

Blues in paintings we collected,
oil on canvas, watercolors, acrylics,
shades of blues like waves keeping us afloat.
Fractured shells, rip-rap, kelp litter
the shores as long as our eyes
focus on ebb and flow.

CAPERS

We call you immature, unripened, dark green
flower buds, in Latin *Capparis spinosa*,
a condiment pickled in vinegar or salt, or both,
here served with bagels and lox. In France
called *petits pois* in a Nicoise salad, in Greece
the size of figs in Santorini.
                              I've seen capers
growing on bushes in Malta seasoning
the rocky shore, their saltiness reminding
of the surrounding sea. The apostle Paul
must have tasted them with bread before
he picked up a wooden stick that turned
into a snake.
                    Brined, dark and moist as
the devil's mind or round like sheep pellets
discovered on a walk in pastoral meadows,
I prefer to call them the caviar
of islands.
                    My husband has learned my love
for capers, sneaks recipes for chicken piccata
or pasta putanesca onto my chair. He knows
how to extract a smile, a sparkle in my eyes.
Give me capers or give me death, he toasts
to our love, the fullness of earth on our tongues,
washed clean with the bubbles of champagne.

VERKLEMPT

Some mornings clouds fill with gloom,
verklempt, choked up, uptight,
the sky as if caught in a vice.

                    I hear *verklempt*,
feel pierced by a hook like an old coat,
my mind forced, squeezed into a metal box
contrary to my usual free fall flying over a sea
of knowledge.

                  I am a lover of butterflies
and hummingbirds, the delicate process of petals
forming into a bloom.

                  In Yiddish *verklempt*
means a man depressed and grieving
at the loss of his brother. I, too,
have known that feeling.

                  Perhaps *verklempt*
stems from *Klammer* in German, verb *klemmen*,
a wooden pin mother used to hang
linens on the line.

                  Some mornings words flap
in the wind. Some mornings they open
the squeaky door to a spacious barn.
They climb to the loft, fall into piles of hay
that scratch and needle the day.

HOUSE POEM

Light spindles a web
around me
as I carve out rooms
for memory and dreams.

Today my imagination
fattens with sky,
an ocean's ebb and flow,
and thousands of years
I walked through history.

In my mouth a wheat field
sways in the wind
and house windows elbow
through the stories.

There is always a halo
of haze on top
of the mountain
where the rooms teeter.

As the house sheds itself,
the field fills itself
with shafts of light,
possibilities for harvest.

INCARCERATED

As if the wick flickered the candle,
the chair took hold of me,
and the pen wrote itself on paper.

It's that kind of morning.
Air bruising leaves.
Blue sky flocking clouds.

The floor stares at the soles
of my shoes, tongue-tied.
Coffee darkens and warms my cup.

I am self-distancing
as the world shuts the door
on a virus that searches for victims.

I am lost in the hour
and the hour ticks inside me.
I am my own clock.

There is no story. I am a blank
page, books grown old with me,
caught in the maze of meaning.

TV and dreams hold my mind
on track number three. Yes,
that's my train.

It rails in the same direction
while the country jails itself,
sends everyone on leave.

Savannah, Georgia

Outside the window the world has turned
enough on its axis to move the day
from dawn-gray to the blue of August.
I see the tangle of live oaks,
bougainvillea mounting the white fence,
hear the waves' rhythm and the steady
shshsh of fan blades overhead.

Time calls me back to Tennessee,
to the old life that is waiting with open arms.
There the house sits quietly
pushed against the knoll,
there the birds' tiny tongues gossip
in branches of sweetgum and sourwood.

I move calmly in that house,
sandaled, heart a soft beat inside me,
windows floor to ceiling
pressing me into the arms of woods.

WATER OR FIRE?

Here twigs and branches litter the garden
after last night's arrival of Harvey's
strongman winds and clouds
plumbed with rain.
Trees bent close to the house,
branches tore off, and leaves let go
in the shuffle.

At the coast, fires rushed the land
and houses as wind celebrated
leaping flames, and earth's riches
fed into the building heat.

Inside we say thanks that the waters
dried off, that the fires grayed and were doused,
that some families returned to their homes.
Others lost this game of chance.

Here trees and roses sigh with relief
in cooling air. Azaleas believe it is spring
early and bloom white like spume
sitting on top of waves.

As if the sea had fallen from heaven,
waves like clouds moan
the days forward, then pull back
at the moon's command.

STURM UND DRANG

Wind stirs bulbous and billowed clouds
    brewing a storm.

Rooms turn the color of pale rum
    as the light changes outside.

Neither dark nor day,
                birds and critters
hunker down like igneous rock
    buried in the woods.
                  Our fingers
wade through litanies of prayer:

    Spare us from the tumult of a twister,
the finesse of the eye clutching
    roofs and lives' stock,
              lifting all
    for a closer look,
            then letting go,
    letting it all fall

into the arms
    of a new world.

Big Bang

Per Henrik Bille
(Acrylic on paper)

The artist offers a ball of chaos,
of movement, that dominates three fourth
of his painting, perhaps offends,
but is balanced by three bold glyphs
stacked along the left-hand side.

Layers of deep rust and brown burst
underneath the tight white net of energy
that controls, prophesies a higher force
above a dense beech forest
where ochre runes run through like rabbits.

The lower right-hand edge raises the outline
of a serpent and within striking distance
the stick figure shadow of pre-historic man.

Bold brush strokes, like arms, reach
from the center of chaos toward the trinity
of symbols, solid like houses built on rock:

First, two orbs like eyes all-seeing,
next the sign for mankind - lesser than -
and last a circle for the sum of all –
an everlasting truth: human longing
destined to fill the God-shaped void.

FINAL DECADE

I will continue to live with gnomes
in the woods, elves in the garden,
and flowers as my grandchildren.

I see the spider walking on water,
the hummingbird following the scents
of petunia and scarlet runner bean vine.

I try to see myself in the smallest way,
in the blue veins on top of my hand,
the callus between my toes.

Branches shed particles of bark.
Dust sits on the window sill.

Who doesn't twitter or facebook
to be heard? The words echo in space.

Earth is just another sphere
like the moon with its craters
and Mars with its dust casting a red hue.

The farther we travel, the smaller we are.
Each of my hairs has been counted,
my name written in His palm.

LANGUAGE OF WALLS

Sometimes walls become curtains
flapping in the breeze,
allowing words to flow through.

Words not meant to be heard.

My dream enters:

> Cotton drifts like snow.
> Dragonflies skim water.
> Wind stirs my paddle.

I touch the wall to steady myself,
a blind woman, ears tuned
to sounds like rain before sleep.

> Plum trees in full bloom.
> Leaves curl and brown at edges.
> Honey bees bitter.

Walls, listen, listen —

> Unthink nights of snow.
> Uncurl leaves to grow like wings.
> Chant for rain and bees.

PHASMATODEA

Stick bug, ghost insect, apparition,
I see you stuck to the siding like a twig.
Did the wind carry you here?
Able to grow new limbs,
to procreate without a male,
I admire your simple structure.

I usually delight in dragon begonias,
their wild orange tongues surging upward
and liriope sending out blue fingers
as if testing air. Why should this bug,
thin and long as a needle,
catch my eye?

Tonight I sit with friends under the striped
awning, toasting another birthday.
Statistics of ten more years to live
cling to me like a phantom limb.
For good luck should I throw
a pinch of salt over my shoulders?

My heart still pumps as I hoist the hours
like stones, stack walls, moan in sleep
as if afraid to die in the branches of a dream.
Does the stick-bug play a song I don't know?
I listen, but hear the sound of an owl
as it spots its prey.

SOLITUDE

Made of quiet and secret things,
stillness of nothing new,
like deer grazing the knoll
in late afternoon light,
shadows thinning their bodies
as if interested only in shapes of night.

Through the window bare branches
in a windless forest, no birds.
Strange what time decides to leave
behind and what it keeps for itself.

This picture of silence, a place
where shadows thrive, where light
gives in and only faith remains.

SOME ARE BLESSED

You live where the trains roll
through midnight, carry produce
to the markets while stars blink
at the moon.
              You pull covers tighter,
return to your mind's reel as the rails
sing a wheeled song.

Pins and needles in your toes you wonder
what do they carry?
              Perhaps love
in a jelly glass you unscrew
                        or happiness,
ribbons you can braid around you?

Your luck lives in a world
that supplies what you need.
                        You toss
and turn, hear doors slam,
metal on metal,
              ratcheting in.

WHEN HISTORY CONVICTS

Let it sink in.
The constant reminder of the sins
of history.
       Not mine.
Slip off that garment of cellophane
clinging to the mind
           universal.
I try to laugh,
        pry this damn thing
off me that keeps burning
my inside.
      I wasn't there.
It happened without me.

Yet everywhere I turn,
even in church,
        someone finds it,
the history,
      and uses it as an example.

Yes, the history of that country
is buried inside me
         with my father.
It clings to my blood,
the sins of the fathers of that time.

How they shaped the years afterwards,
all the sharp-edged slivers left
the preacher throws at me.

I've prayed that history will be
forgiven.
        I've prayed.

III.

Natural Selection

To be a branch that lifts and grows
toward the sky as waxy-white blooms
open to lemony scents.

To be striped roots of crepe myrtle
snaking toward the stone terrace,
furred with moss, like words
years have forgotten.

To be bleeding hearts blossoming
with yellow stamen next to lilies
of the valley, breathing in fragrance,
lingering in the love of bells.

To laugh like a bell, clear and sweet,
or be the branch that bends in rain,
soaks in songs of wings,
the gentle brush of a feather.

Like love that quietly slides between
sticks and stones and disappears
in the maze of laurel and sourwood.

Survival of the fittest, the blood's surge
seeking otherness. Words that retreat
into a glass globe someone will shake.

Name Calling

The first time I was called a *Kraut*
after arriving in Tennessee, I laughed

remembering the cabbage mother cooked
with onions, apples, and a wurst.

Once a week she bought Kraut
at Thursday's market, sliced hot potatoes

over cabbage and wurst on my plate,
steam curling to my nose.

My sister and I swallowed happiness,
held on to it like hunger.

A Time As This

Knobby tips of the lilac tree wait patiently
for the next rain to open their eyes
when overhead clouds spill
as heaven's power pushes down.

I listen to the language trees and shrubs
speak or the mountains proclaim,
of the creek rolling through
the neighborhood after a week's rain.

I watch and listen through the windows,
bide time, mark off the calendar,
hear, learn, and repeat all the new words
like a parrot: Social distancing,
alone together, shelter-in-place.

As the future reclines in a chair,
the screen explains half-life –
difficult for the young who never knew
a time when they couldn't leave the house
or buy their wishes.

I think of my German mother who raised
five children through six years of World War II,
when a loaf of bread and bone soup shared
and digging potatoes at night was the norm.

A time as this is easy for me when I play
Beethoven, each note's tiny lobe dancing
on the lines or I read Rilke, words
transforming into a poem.
All the time to change fear into hope.

The Garden

I've begun looking on weeds as flowers,
burrs climbing the stems,
heart-shaped leaves imitating the hours
I fill with heat-burned holes
as I shed loose living and noisy news.
laugh about prison reality shows.
It is human to seek pleasure.

I am half weed, half flower,
snappish with moments of bud
and bloom. Spirits linger inside
the rustle and breaking of twigs
as I walk through the last days,
avoid bee hives and bogs, steady
my feet on rip-rap, orient myself
to the sun, the moon, and the stars
just like all women,
                    gathering.

INVITATION

Scraping corn for soup
my hands weaken as I grasp
the knife and the cob.

I add kernels to broth
seasoned with celery, onion, parsley,
stir in a cornstarch slurry,
squirts of cream,
whisk it into a summer soup.

Each bite a taste of growth
from seed to stalk to tasseled husk
as I have grown into my final shape,
learned to speak the language of love,
a boiled-down liquid of muscle, marrow,
and blood, its bones and gristle.

Come swallow the components
broken down in the mouth.
Taste the acerbic, the milky kernels,
the sweet in the end. Sop up soup
with a slice of daily bread,
a pinch of earth's salt.

INTERLUDE

The year has swallowed two seasons
of adjustments to a new normal
the wind blew across the globe.
Not like snow or rain,
but like a shroud that frayed
and chose its new wearers.
We never again can claim innocence
to hug and kiss, shake hands
or give high-fives.
Our hearts learn a new music,
reserved, like a symphony conducted
on the radio. We learn
to translate love into words
that will slake our thirst for touch.
We were created to cling to each other,
to hold each other up,
to gather in twos or more.
The world teases us out of meaning.
Where does that leave us?
So far the earth is still round,
the house has not collapsed,
and this season will give way to another.
It has always been this way.
Fat years turn to lean.
Without rain, drought sets in.
This is an interlude to the next phase:
We are gifts to one another.

WINDOW TO THE DAY

Roses plump themselves with hope,
the opening of small businesses and good will
during a pandemic.

Summer can't wait much longer
as it begins to form buttons and fists
collecting blooms until they burst.

I watch a female cardinal feeding,
then flying a seed to the male.
Sealed with this kiss,
they fly away together.

I am cleaning off shelves,
want to rid myself of doo-dads and knick-knacks,
but not having the heart to toss them.
Memories, however small,
treasures.

My life hidden in miniature folds.
I need to let go of the past like a sigh of wind
as the universe spins silk into stars
across the evening sky,
calls me to rise.

Worm Moon

Sated with the sun's sheen, the full moon
wakens all that lies beneath earth.

Courage, women say to each other
in the face of trouble. Bear up.
They sprinkle chicken soup with turmeric,
drink ginger tea, take two teaspoons
of black elderberry syrup to boost
the immune system.

Like a barn standing at the roadside
I open my doors offering
a loaf of daily bread and shade inside
after a day's heat.

CLOUDS

They never fail to tell us rain is in the air.
They synchronize with the wind that strokes
and cajoles their shoulders until they let go
of their cargo.
           Today, the sun prevails
and they seceded like the South to the North,
left the sky as blue as cornflowers in a field.

I dream in cumulonimbus,
see Max Schmeling readying for a bout,
Romeo and Juliet kissing, or Ariel
diving into the sea of blue.
           The Grimm Brothers
must have pictured Haensel and Gretel
in clouds as drops of rain bewitched them,
left wispy strands of cirrus or nimbostratus,
released flakes, covered the tips of spruce
in the Black Forest where *Heinzelmaennchen*
or kind trolls in their pointed green hats
cooked a meal for honest farm wives.

I grew up with clouds as they changed
their stories. Without them we'd have no rain,
no snow, no shield from the sun
or for the moon to hide and seek.
           I remember

standing in the *Piazza San Marco*
and a sudden downpour scattered tourists
eating pizza or linguini in red sauce,
turning over tables.
                  I have seen the Liberty Bell
in clouds since the fourth grade when we had to
recite *Die Glocke* by Friedrich Schiller,
how it was burned out of clay.
                        William Turner
also watched the sky each day at Covent Garden.
He knew clouds intimately, their scale and shape,
painted clouds and the light they could swallow
or expose.

Outpouring of Self

The future enters into us, in order
to transform itself in us,
long before it happens.

Rainer Maria Rilke

While the coffee machine stutters black brew
in the kitchen, the hose curls on pavers
surrounding the pool, and the king snake
raises her head, spits her tongue at you
before you broom it into the woods.

You breathe easier now that order is restored,
not the garage nesting the king snake,
not the kitchen brewing in the coffee machine,
not the morning watching you scream.
Only the immortals survive in the dimension
between times, gliding up and down the scales
of the heart's song the future plays inside you.

You love the earth with its voices: The train's whistle,
the rush of cars on the freeway, the dog's bark
next door. And in the woods, the crackle
of branches falling, the rustle of underbrush
as a family of deer leap through,
but the serpent nestles between roots.

Somehow the future waits inside you
to connect to the day,
laid in front of you, stuttering,
curling, spitting, an outpouring of self,
blood and water, raising goosebumps –
not what you expected –
you shrinking away from the future like a bird
eying a cat below the feeder.

Variation on a Theme by Rainer Maria Rilke

We cannot know what Michelangelo sculpted
into David with eyes the depth of a pine forest,

the torso, filled with sweetness the size
of a honeycomb. His stance muscled, sinewed,

hands larger than expected, perhaps holding
the dreams of a sculptor, the birds he cups

at night but fly away at morning. His torso
remembers the chisel that formed his hips

and thighs wished of any lover. The marble
sheen of his flesh glinting like the Milky Way

of a million stars. We cannot count how often
admirers stroked his shoulders and blushing

touched the member of stone, hewn out
of a mountain stacked for centuries with rain,

sun, and the *Schmutz* of the world. Can any
human change his life to such perfection?

Autumn Pastoral

The house looms like a lion
that growls and snaps
clenched air. How small the room
where I breathe. Even smaller
the chair I sit in for hours.

But I'm not angered by this smallness
invading me. I hoard the sun's rays
caught in leaves,
drink the shadows of trees.

I watch thin spiders seeking refuge
in corners and the dust of stars
settling in eaves. Stillness gasps
between sill and lintel.

Poetry and a cup of pale wine
mute the times masking egos
as news pummels and stings like hail.
Ancient stones cool the fevered body.

The flutes of autumn blow a pastoral
and the woods speak. They feed
the soul and tangled dreams
while the face of the moon,
white as a ghost,
watches the house shift.

WINDSWEPT

The moon's footprint lights the study, rests
over Goethe and Rilke where I left the myth
of my heart, love and loss, those fires not yet
extinguished. On lone evenings like this
I sit and warm myself on thin flames that leap,
listen to the soft words repeated as they long
for the season when trees birth leaves, reach.
I should let go but hold on to the last song
the flames sing. Come sit with me by the pyre
that slowly dwindles to embers. Since the past
doesn't fit anymore, flick its rags into the fire
seasoned with the salt and sour of days passed,
let it die in the whiffs of wind, and let the lies
disappear into this night like fireflies.

RILKE'S SWAN

What savvy spider wove a web
touching azalea to hemlock
that root toward the pond?

A swan sails along the edge
while morning sun imprints
his snowy wings with gold.

Fractions of light divide the pond
into a water puzzle the swan
solves nearly weightlessly.

I envy his apparent simple life,
head held high, forgetting
his awkward walk on land.

When from the porch the pond
lies still and serene, the swan
has scribed poems onto water.

THE GIFT – JUNE 5

– for Lauren

Born to create
            you threw the clump of clay
you dug from the garden when burying
canna bulbs for summer
                        against the garage floor,
a thud, thud, thud,
                  until it softened enough
to be molded.

I watched you wedge the clay,
knead, fold, knead,
as shrubs and trees depend on the sun's climb,
and as it passed the house
                        a cup shaped itself
between your fingers
                  with a handle and a top
to keep a liquid hot.

You held it in your hands like a fledgling
fallen from a nest,
                  your mind wild,
a sun curling grass in summer,
as if a small god had come to earth
to show me the miracle of creating
a vessel out of dirt.

You fired the cup, glazed it, fired it again,
holding now the memory of you,
the entire day.
        No wheel and pedal
to control the shape,
            you molded love,
a spade-full of earth,
into a vessel that could be filled.

SLANTED MORNING

Crepe Myrtles divide the day
into grey strips and blotches.

Wind rattles the house
and windows square a pool.

Rain swallows the sky.

The pool's lip is paved
with footprints of raccoons.

The kitchen chains light,
says, *you again.*

Light strings between steps.

Counters scatter bits
of leftovers like a rash.

The door opens to a wide patch
denying grass a home.

Nothing is spared from prayer.

KATZENJAMMER

A mother named her baby Lucifer,
      a connotation of evil incited
            each time she calls his name –

like the phosphorescence of a firefly
      calls death beautiful
            as it lights up

The shape love can take –

      the housecat birthing kittens
            in an abandoned chair
               in the attic

      a maybug kept in a matchbox
            lined in new leaves
               and rose petals

a black butterfly,
      wings edged in lapis,
            harnessed by a scent,

a promise of love,
      as it siphons droplets of broth
            from my sandal.

Luna Moth

When I saw you again, homeless,
blending into the light-grey of the house,
your viridescent wings held flat against
the siding, I spoke to you with tenderness
as if I saw an old friend after two years.
You did not move, just took in my words,
your painted eyes cast down, already losing
perspective in your one-day world.
Are you an omen? A portent to hold on?
You've come so far to press your tiny soul
against the house, grasping what I as well
cling to in storms that lash and rasp nagging
the walls, our breaths leaving tiny trails
that still hinge us to life.

READING MOLL FLANDERS

Because the wooden stairs climb
from the pool to the house
with the lithe movement of a tiger,
because spent flowers dangle
from their hanging pots like wire
trying to untangle, because
you woke from a dream,
you opened the book
and all the words were you.
You are the story.

The sky is Adonis blue.
Moll walks through a field of poppies
like suitors that spread in front of her.
Because the flowers murmur
promises, she binds them into
a bouquet. Black stamen –
bright-red petals.

She holds them in her hands
like proposals
she accepts.
But each time she gives in
to love, the sky grays,
clouds bunch and rain
breezes cool air.
She shivers.

When she arrives at the story's back door,
the poppies hang their heads
and her hem drips puddles.
The door is locked.
She never finds the key that turns
to happiness. The last
page is dimpled and smeared
because the story
that is yours
dies in rags, not riches.

FALSE ALARM

for Nick

Roused by the Medical Alert call
from my first sleep, I expected
to see you prone on the floor
or worse suspended over
the kitchen sink, water pouring
onto the floor when I rushed
through your door. The room
lit by the moon full in the window
I called your name. Only silence.
I found you toweling off in the tub
with a surprised look *What? How?*
You didn't push the button?
No!
Well then, all is ok and I'll leave.
Sure, come back another time.

Keeping Your Enemy Close

Cooped up at home so long it is easy
for my neighbor to drape his pet snake
around his arm, take it for an open-window
drive through town. He says,
Oscar likes to hang around,
the python's head poised in the breeze.

I remember Genesis
where God cursed the serpent:
Dust you will eat.

My neighbor says, *it's a pet,*
a companion for lonely nights
winding its way through my dreams,
dragging dust motes from room to room.

He jaunts away
and I turn to my garden's fig tree,
its large leaves hiding
marble-sized green fruit ripening
birds, squirrels, and I covet.

My neighbor is a courageous man
to keep what God cursed so close,
to live and breathe with each day.

THE OPEN GATE

Trees are poems the earth writes upon the sky
          – Kahlil Gibran

Lilac buds test spring air.
Yoshino cherry trees cloud the yard
in soft pink, look like women blooming
tulle tufts, lace ruffles, fringes,
as earth rhythms each line.

We count our days and years in trees,
those tender stirrings of beginnings,
glorious leavings and flowerings
in our prime, the slow dying
before we enter the next life.

In childhood chestnut trees called
our sponge-like spirits to create.
Candled blooms, velvety brown fruit
we strung into tribal neck coverings.
Cherry trees' succulent red orbs transcended
to ornaments we hung over our ears.

I've seen love flow through trees
growing close, leaning in,
winding arms around each other,
becoming one as branches intertwined,
burst into a leafy crown.

Trees pulse and throb growing circles.
Their roots probe and explore earth,
hold our spirit tendrils beneath bark,
open the gate to poetry, its sudden shudders,
those delicate tremblings
when an arrow hits its mark.

WHAT WE DON'T GIVE UP

Immigrant.
          Alien.
I gave up my fatherland,
my mother tongue,
denied what ancestors groomed
into conversations,
wanting to belong,
to speak as mother said,
with a hot potato in your mouth.

I became a copycat
wishing to blend in,
drank new words like swigs of sweet tea
running through me,
cooling, exhilarating,
pushing me into the midst
of the American South.
                    Foreigner.
I was a hummingbird
sampling flowery expressions,
melodies of speech,
ya'll come see us,
swear words.
          Stranger in a strange land

prying a way
through the streets of freedom.
I gave up father's lost war,
mother's cooking,
collected recipes
for fried chicken, cornbread,
apple pie.

But on evenings
when rain washes the windows,
I form my mouth around words
in mother's cookbook
written in old-script German,
Gefuellter Hefezopf,
Linsensuppe,
Dampfnudeln,
            the way she used to.

IV.

NAMED

My sister, Gerlinde, named for the Linden tree
the ancients worshipped as earth mother.
Townspeople gathered underneath
heart-shaped leaves, dense crown in summer,
strong-branched in winter,
deep-rooted in all seasons.

I was named Helga, a Nordic name, meaning
holy. Why not a good old German name
like my sister's, Brunhilde, Irmgard,
or Waltraud in an Aryan war?
I had to step out of my country to live
by my name. It sits briefly on the tongue,
leaving the mouth open for meaning.

Once named, you must follow the name,
your name, to the end.

GIRL WITH PURPLE BALLOON

Brandi Donan
(oil on canvas)

Legs splayed, bending forward,
she clasps the balloon as if it were filled
with wishes, floating
like a dove
through her childhood,
pinafore and ponytail ruffling air.

Sitting like this on the ground,
she seems weighted down
by the purple orb of life,
strife and grief,
bursting over her head
at any time.

Surely, she will learn to let go.

MIRROR OF TIME

Above the hills, thin trails of nimbus
visible, two hours past midnight,
October 31, when the world saves time
and money.

The poet forgets about time,
has no money, but lives in a world
of words still ruminating within,
ricocheting,

phrases turned over in sleep,
formulating a line, then returning
to the wheel of sleep that ratchets
through a childhood in the Black Forest,
time spent in Berlin, Siena, or Sarajevo,
on the bridge where Franz Ferdinand
was killed, always ending in the arms
of someone dead but born anew.

The poet scrubs and empties the niches
of memory that frown, heal, or soften the face
while counting the coins of riches
paid by each one.

The days will be longer the news tells
but no vaccine yet for the coronavirus.
More guns stolen than before,
the yellow lights of parking lots no deterrent.

The past mirrors time for the future,
its reflection mere shadow play.

THE TRAPEZE ARTIST

When you scatter the ash of our past
in front of my feet, I step over it,
remember swinging on the trapeze
of love and drinking the sugar-rimmed cup
of first days. Months percolated
between us like fresh-brewed coffee
before the poison of carelessness
slowly slipped in, convicted our desires
and exiled them to a country
I will never see again.
                         But after rain,
the air is like a poem about the past,
white-washed, slaking each leaf,
each flower with a blessing
that empowers the wren to build
her nest amid impatiens
in the window box, that resurrects
the now dead dressed in movie finery
to bring joy in the free fall
without a safety net.

DEMENTIA

As if you stood on top
            of Mount Everest looking
        out on a sea
of clouds, you stopped in the middle
            of the kitchen,   envelope
                in hand, lost
for the word for the tool
        you looked for.
                            You walked
            the alphabet forward
from A,   perused the D's waiting
        on your mind's assembly line,
then the M's   until you landed
            on S.
    Was it sugar?
        You took a step back, stopped
and *school* came to mind.
                            No.
You breathed a long sigh of disgust,
        finally asked
                    your husband,
        What do you use to open
                an envelope?
He said,
The long side of a pen or a strong finger.
                No. No,

you answered,
                    something sharper.
Shafts of light parted the clouds,
synapses fired,
                    and scissors
            popped into your head.

Much later another thought came to you.
You could have used a knife.

IMAGE

I tossed the years over my shoulder
like a pinch of salt.
My neighbor wasn't so lucky.
She wears the wrinkled mask of age
and I am shocked. She must have fallen
into the pit of grief and worry,
unable to shed their cloaks.
I sit by the window, watch trees shoot up
and the garden grow over with weeds.
But the sun, the moon, and I are the same.
Stars are born to die.
I refuse to heed the commands of earth,
twirl through rooms like a ballerina.
My neighbor is bent over a walker.
I treat my limbs like old friends
with sweet creams and potions.
My neighbor can't lift a spoon
to feed herself, can't dress herself.
Her pockets are torn,
refuse to hold the house keys.
Her mouth is pressed like a flower in a book
as she is taken away.
I don't look into the mirror anymore.
It lies shamelessly.

HOMILY

Snowflakes hunker in clouds, each stamped
     with a star design. I smell their cool,
clear fragrance in air as I pour bird seeds
     in the feeder, hear the cardinal announcing
breakfast.
       This is the church of routines,
the credo, the eucharist, and the blessing.
     Squirrels kneel in anticipation, wrens splash
in holy water.
       I am the priest in ornate vestments
presenting the host for the taking.
               Around us
flakes fall like little angels, covering us before they melt
into feathers and cloak.
       I am guided today
to cup the luck of a cricket chirping
in a warm corner of the house.

Will the flutter of wings stir another storm
     or is it simply a reminder that I am watched?
Will I end the day as saint fighting my halo
     every step?

BLESSINGS, STILL

I have given up the moon
for a night light. Given up symphonies
for simple songs, formal gardens
for a single bloom.

Trees give up their leaves,
flowers their blooms.
Days give up light for dark.

But moss clings to the bank,
stones huddle, and your eyes
still love me.

Our island is still large enough
for a cup of rain as the shore pools
the sea at our feet, and kelp
washes its hair in sand.

OVER THERE

– for Anneliese Hodapp

It is noon in Oberkirch.
The husband calls to his wife,
but she just lies there,
smiling at the ceiling.
The sun plays with shadows.
Roses blush the garden window.
Soup on the stove burbles
like a brook.

The husband phones
their daughters, their son.

Soft rain soothes the hour.

They are still a family as long
as they hold each other,
until the mortician carries his wife,
their mother, to her shadow.

They will live in her absence
awakening needs,
her laughter puzzling
the tablecloth
forever flowering roses.

MITGEFUEHL

I was shocked seeing you
in the priest's hands.
A few handfuls of ashes
in an urn. You
who fed and led me,
who loved me.

Your heart, filled with war,
divorce, poverty,
and disappointments
finally said, *enough*.

I will place you in a niche
like a relic. Your slivers
of bone holy.

I will say your name
to my children,
and they will say it
to their children.
I will pass your name
around a table of friends
until they repeat it.

Your name will rise
to the clouds that gather
and spread over the sky.
They will darken
and rumble your name
through valleys
and in mountains
that echo
          mother, mother,
    other . . .

Sorrow

A hickory nut, shell encasing fruit
that whorls inside us. A lump
sitting in the chest sending roots
through the body that wind around
the marrow of bones, stifle breath.
We cling to it when loss falls
over us like snow, melts into us,
then hardens the consistency of stones.

Here, by the roadside, we mourn loss
we have to bury, see it as a well
from which we draw water in pails.
Evenings we sit inside
and learn to live with sorrow.
We stretch and fold it like linen,
stack it in a closet.

TESTIMONY

Like Rilke, I call on angels straddling stars
to carry my words on cold white wings
through the Milky Way.

Last night we listened to Bach,
sacrificed our sorrows
and the wheel of wishful thinking
as the notes flowed through the room.

The old stories whisper inside me.
The caves, stalactites hanging like cork screws
from their domes, the boys lost.

Remember.

The brother and sister we loved
and gave back to earth.

Wall after wall of sadness crumbles
in my mouth. I remember, the huddle
of warmth from your body,
the fire dwindling slowly.

The rose unfolding her petals, the basket of guile,
the prickly hide of the hedgehog,
all testimony we were a part of,
the open door, our footsteps,

remember.

Remember to rescue the flicker
from ashes and smoke.

LEAVES OF LIFE

The season of fog lies over the valley.
    When I look down, I'm standing
at the shore of an ancient sea,
    waiting for the boat to arrive.
If I listen hard, I can hear the slashing
    of oars, measuring the distance
between us. Two worlds that overlap.
    One that is reality and one
we create for ourselves. One is on fire,
    the other extinguished, numbed.

Expeditions to Iona uncovered the Book of Kells,
    in Wittenberg the Bible Luther translated
from Aramaic into the common German language.
    The Scriptures seen like leaves of life,
carefully deciphered and collected.
    Each word an eye on the future,
on the coming.

Life is like the carving of coral into a necklace
    that fits, that we can admire
in the mirror, that, if we squint, expands
    into the salt pans of Sicily, all rosy pink
if the sun sparks and lightens it.

Trees waited all day for the wind
    to touch them, but this morning
Japanese maple leaves are strewn
    like anise stars over the terrace.

A New Day Rises

Outside the open door of the blue-grey house
the cardinal calls perched in sweet gum,
sunflower seeds poured in the feeder.
He is messenger of joy,
red feathers like flares winging air,
a go-ahead light for the day.

Giant-leafed hostas unfold for summer,
blue salvia remembers last year's abundance,
and liriope ruffles green and white striped
skirts. Daylilies clasp tight little fists
in preparation for blooming days.

Inside drifts of hope for traveling
without restrictions whisper,
flutter to the surface like light lifted,
all created for you,
but others live this day
in the eternal world.

As the sun turns away from earth,
this day is like a secret chamber in space,
shadowed. Yet roses open folds,
cardinals feed and mate,
petunias flourish in the window box.
When the opened door closes behind you
and light changes to shadows,
the river will carry you through.

THE LAST TURN

Air tart as a slice of lemon,
two crows bicker in sweetgums,
turn my face up, frowning.

This morning mists the garden
as I empty the pool skimmer
packed with fallen leaves,
let the water breathe again.

Reading that heart and lungs weaken
after illness, will never be the same,
fear sits in me, the afflicted.

My hour will come hobbling over stones,
carry shadows I've never seen before
to a path through thistle.

I sit by the fire, listen to the crackle of wood,
watch the flames as they scribe
the tree of life.

I spool the day's threads onto a bobbin.
Who can tell which turn is the last?

NOT YET WINTER

I am the glitter on the crust of the snow
N. Scott Momaday

Wind tilts birches, spins leaves silver.
I hurry down the acorn-littered driveway.
A deer leaps into bushes and disappears.

Fall marched in like a warrior
as wind tugs at robe and hair.
Mums golden in the window box.

Flower of life not yet wilted,
I turn my back on the weather,
light a candle for prayer.

Once my soul leaves the body
will I live between sheetrock and studs
or will I be banished to leap over clouds,
glide on the shoulders of winds?

Ghosts rise in the flicker,
whisper my name.
I shut my eyes to the bones of the day,
wish to return in snowflakes
melting into you,
crusting your chest with glitter.

READING THE OBITUARIES

You look at their photos, one young, the other old,
and wonder about the years in between.
The ones that carried the fine details
of a life.

She had odd jobs,
such as DoorDash, and set up yard sales.

He loved his garden,
when spring flamed the azaleas
or when fall crowned the maple in gold,
and was an extremely hard worker.

She was a riveter at Lockheed.
He drove a forklift for over 40 years.

Imagine the understories:
The day her pan of oil caught fire.
The day he was voted chairman of the board
and ogled the new secretary.
The time her girdle slipped to her breasts
when she ran through the rain.

The day his wife wanted blackberries
for a pie and they got caught in a patch
of poison ivy.
They must have laughed about it later.

You won't ever know all the details,
the emotions, the refusals, the days of pure love.

When you listen to people who've reached 100,
he might say, *I took a swig of whiskey each morning,*
or *I ate biscuits and bacon every day,*
or she says, *I gardened and prayed.*

They marked off each day on their calendar of life,
went to sleep or fell into a coma
and never woke,
their souls a mountain stream
digging into the banks, flowing along.

BARELY AUDIBLE

No one sees or hears what happens
when the soul leaves and re-enters the body
as darkness settles in each corner
of the room and the moon rises over
the house. Absence of time finds me
perusing the shelves stocked with wishes,
when my soul meets with yours in dreams
confirming our needs. This is when the leaves
of our hearts deepen and blood rushes through.
Only the first clouded light of dawn reveals
the leaves have fluttered to the ground,
barely audible. Wakened, early winds shuffle
their tiny shadows into a moon dance,
a catch of breath behind my throat.

END OF NOVEMBER

The driveway is littered with the mast of hickory trees,
half-shells of nuts that crunch and wedge themselves
in the bottom of your soles. Squirrels want to keep
the nuts a secret, line their dens, hide others quietly.

Feeling the cool air on my short-sleeved arms,
I sense a melancholy as I see some leaves have fallen,
curl on the garden floor like wrens.

Summer let go of hibiscus with its crimson
plate-sized blooms, blue-tailed lizards sunning on rocks,
yet when I see my face in the mirror, the years lie
in wrinkles and folds gracefully, Southern-like.

Preparing dinner, I watch a raccoon family
grazing bird feeder droppings, taking a drink
in the pool next to pyracantha that already grows
orange berries, a sign of fall.

We live with falling, giving in, giving way, letting go.
Haven't we died to the self already many times
as we learned life?

Here the world and its ways will end for me,
but the trees and the house will breathe
my thoughts, memories, the little miracles.
They will tell all if you listen.

BAKING BREAD

Not only white but whole wheat mixed in,
white and brown ground seeds of earth,
a slurry of yeast that flowers, blooms,
a bit like life.
              Kneaded and fisted, looping
the body around itself, letting it rise.
                                Let it rise
into its own shape as the world weakens
the body, as the body tenses and fights back,
as time between body and world blurs.

In the end, the perfectly rounded shape
pleasing the eye, a plump loaf,
a slice of life we bite into, soothing our hearts.

Slightly acrid this learning, kneading, fisting
each day, looping around years,
opening the mind for afterlife, a way
that allows us to leave earth,
                    allows us to rise.

Tornado Warning January 2020

– for Brandi and Eric

No chasm between our houses
only pines and deciduous trees
as the radar blipped severe storms
that would bend bare branches
like dancers in a staged ballet.

The air was heavy and still
as if a spring day awakened
forsythia and azalea to bloom.
Birds and squirrels power-fed
earlier, nestled in their beds.

Finally wind and thunder rushed
the trees. Rain loosened
the last leaves. Lightning flashed
the darkening sky.

Phones and TV alerted us
to take cover. Our neighbor texted:
The shelter has enough room
and we have wine
and a movie we can play.

This morning only one tree fell
between our houses, roots pointing
to the sky like a giant hand thankful
for neighbors without fences.

WHAT IF

the camelias, their red-hot blooms
    were meant to teach us
that they will dry and fall off
    like little pale fists,
that their fallen fists will feed birds
    that flit through the garden
hugging their feathers tightly.
What if we think
of the ancients huddling around
    the discovery of fire
like birds rushing the feeder,
    flames lapping stale cave air,
smoke wafting around their shoulders
    like a warming blanket
in a world they had to learn.
    What if the wild ox, boar, buck
taught them their A, B, C's for history,
    gnawing bones to the marrow,
the arithmetic of counting on fingers
    the words they mouthed
and remembered for survival, that
    twigs rubbed together
and branches the women gathered
    would start and sustain the fire.

RETURN TO THE BLACK FOREST

On track seven, dank cabin smell invites
the past –
        steel wheels on rails vibrating
        oak benches,
                steam hissing
        past windows like ghosts.

A whistle blows.

In velveteen seat I listen to the smooth clickety-click
that glides me past fir and spruce,
the Black Forest.

I speed through tunnels, the losses,
                winged souls
      floating in and out of me,
              smoky
like these stacked stone openings
built into the mountains.

I remember the lean years after World War II,
      walks to kindergarten
              squeezing
    my sister's hand,
          my school days,
milk powder treats,
        evenings, my head heavy

on the kitchen table

               waiting for mother to return,
worn from the factory.

The train slows and stops in my home town.
Our church bell rings noon,

                  delivers me

to the day when I left.

WHEN WINTER CALLS

Crocheting time I watch the clock
on the window sill beside the terrarium,
your birthday gift, next to a porcelain bird
pecking half an acorn.

                                If I wedge the half shell
between two fingers and blow into the cavity,
you will hear a sharp whistle
as if I were lost.

                        Pulling each loop of blue yarn
through other stitches for hours,
an island of self emerges,

                             like Easter Island,
where monuments of the dead listen
to the moon's fullness as it falls
on their faces looking on their own graves
in the dark, the loss of a tribe,

                                    or an ancient city,
Jerusalem, where faith walked with me
through stone-cobbled streets

                           reminding
of the town crowned by an 11th century castle ruin
I left after twenty-one years.

                         I remember
one school day I chose to pick a basket
of blackberry leaves in nearby woods
for tea brewed in India

                         instead of leaning

at the kitchen table over a math problem
only the teacher understood.

Tiny ferns continue to grow toward the light
that presses each morning through the panes
as my knees lock and my neck stiffens.
The bluebird always bends
to peck the halved acorn
I can turn into an alarm,

                     a whistle,
that would rush you to me.

Is this what is left, a still life
hovering on the sill
of the window to the world?

ELEMENTAL

We exclaim, *no time like this, give me more time,*
it's time to go, as if we could manipulate time,
that eternal measurement of life.

We can stare into the forest for hours, listen
to the wind's sighs in trees, nodding leaves.
Time pools around us, carries away the day.

Time has a wicked streak, is fickle, slows down
as we wait for a son to finish living in a cell,
for a daughter to refuse the needle of bliss.

The seasons know all about time, the right time
for one to spring forward, the other to fall back,
but the wrong time to turn a cold shoulder on need.

We can see time grin in the window of a plane
as we pass the line between night and day,
float by in clouds that pillow around us.

Breathe and believe this is your time to be you.
Watch how time opens doors, shuts them.
Time will never come again,
                                        like this.

NOTES:

Page 3 Loewengasse – Lion's Alley

Page 8 Fleischwurst – Meat Sausage

Page 46 Verklempt – Choked up, uptight

Page 52 Sturm und Drang – Storm and Stress

Page 83 Katzenjammer – Cat's complaint / qualms of conscience

Page 92 Gefuellter Hefezopf – filled yeast braid
         Linsensuppe – lentil soup
         Dampfnudeln – steamed dumplings

Page 106 Mitgefuehl – Compassion

Acknowledgements:

Thank you to the editors who printed these poems.

Abyss and Apex: "After the War"
American Diversity Report: "First Flight"
Amethyst Review: "Poetry"
Artemis: "Invitation"
Avocet: "Rilke's Swan," "Every Breath is a Gift," "End of November," "Not Yet Winter,"
Bluepepper: Incarcerated
Conestoga Zen: "House Poem," "Blessings Still," "Luna Moth"
Heartland Review: "The Open Gate"
Muddy River Poetry Review: "False Alarm"
Poetry Quarterly: "Tornado Warning January 2020"
Sheila-Na-Gig: "Some are Blessed"
Silver Blade: "Stepping Through the Self"
South Florida Review: "Over There"
Sublunary Review: "Barely Audible"
Trouvaille Review: "Natural Selection"
Wild Roof Journal: "Bruised"

Anthologies:

Mizmor Anthology: "A Time as This"
Pandemic Puzzle Poems: "Autumn Pastoral"

"Stepping Through the Self" was nominated for the Pushcart Prize
"Reading Moll Flanders" won the Chattanooga Writers Guild 1st Prize

Thank you also to Diane Frank for publication of this collection and thank you to the people who inspired me to write these poems and who were willing to help me shape them into their final version: KB Ballentine, Chris Wood, Finn Bille (a fellow immigrant), Rachel Crumble, Cynthia Young, Karen Phillips, Wes Sims (members of my Thursday writing group), and John Mannone.

Thank you to Rodney Charles for the design of this book.

Thank you to my husband who encourages my writing and shares the classics.

Besonderen Dank geht an Ursula Spissinger und Johanna Graupe fuer ihre Hilfe bei der Zusammenfassung dieser Kollektion.

About the Author

Helga Kidder is a native of Germany's Black Forest region and now lives in the Tennessee hills with her husband. She was awarded an MFA in Writing from Vermont College. She is co-founder of the Chattanooga Writers Guild and leads one of their poetry groups. She has participated in workshops in San Francisco, CA, Rockvale, TN, and Auvillar, France. Her poems have been published in many journals and anthologies. She was nominated for a Pushcart Prize and has four previous poetry collections, *Wild Plums* (2012) Finishing Line Press, *Luckier than the Stars* (2013) Blue Light Press, *Blackberry Winter* (2016) Blue Light Press, *Loving the Dead* (2020) which won the Blue Light Press Book Award 2020.

www.ingramcontent.com/pod-product-compliance
Lightning Source LLC
Chambersburg PA
CBHW031853090426
42741CB00005B/480